W9-AAE-504

Amazing Animal Skills

SCREAMS AND SONGS
HOW ANIMALS COMMUNICATE TO SURVIVE

ROBIN KOONTZ

mc Marshall Cavendish
Benchmark
New York

Special thanks to Donald E. Moore III, associate director of animal care at the Smithsonian Institution's National Zoo, for his expert reading of this manuscript.

Other Marshall Cavendish Offices: Marshall Cavendish International (Asia) Private Limited, 1 New Industrial Road, Singapore 536196 • Marshall Cavendish International (Thailand) Co Ltd. 253 Asoke, 12th Flr, Sukhumvit 21 Road, Klongtoey Nua, Wattana, Bangkok 10110, Thailand • Marshall Cavendish (Malaysia) Sdn Bhd, Times Subang, Lot 46, Subang Hi-Tech Industrial Park, Batu Tiga, 40000 Shah Alam, Selangor Darul Ehsan, Malaysia

Marshall Cavendish is a trademark of Times Publishing Limited

All websites were available and accurate when this book was sent to press.

Library of Congress Cataloging-in-Publication Data
Koontz, Robin Michal.
Screams and songs : how animals communicate to survive / by Robin Koontz.
p. cm. — (Amazing animal skills)
Includes bibliographical references and index.
Summary: "An exploration of animals who use special skills, such as singing and making other distinct noises, in order to survive"—Provided by publisher.
ISBN 978-0-7614-4907-2 (print)   ISBN 978-1-60870-600-6 (ebook)
1. Animal communication—Juvenile literature. I. Title.
QL776.K66 2012
591.59—dc22
2010016875

EDITOR: Joy Bean   PUBLISHER: Michelle Bisson
ART DIRECTOR: Anahid Hamparian   SERIES DESIGNER: Kristen Branch

Photo research by Joan Meisel
Cover photo: Tohoku Color Agency/Getty Images
The photographs in this book are used by permission and through the courtesy of: *Alamy*: Tom Uhlman, 1, 3, 12(t); Martin Dembinsky Photo Associates, 6; Arco Images GmbH, 7, 38; Terry Whittaker, 8; A & J Visage, 9; Michele Burgess, 18; First Light, 28; Don Johnston, 30; Gerry Pearce, 37(t); Wildlife GmbH, 40; SCPhotos, 42. *Animals Animals-Earth Scenes*: McDonald Wildlife Photog., 21. *Corbis*: Steve Austin/Papilio, 12(b); Photolibrary, 20; Hans Reinhard, 25; Karl Ammann, 34; Stephen Frink, 41. *Getty Images*: Andy Rouse, 14; Georgette Douwma, 31; Martin Harvey, 33. *Minden Pictures*: Michael & Patricia Fogden, 13. *Shutterstock*: Patsy A. Jacks, 4. *SuperStock*: age fotostock, 37(b).

Printed in Malaysia (T)
1 3 5 6 4 2

CONTENTS

CHAPTER ONE

SOUND OFF!

Animals of all kinds communicate in different and often amazing ways. Animals in the air, land, and sea use sound, vibration, chemicals, color, light, and even electrical currents as ways

A Tasmanian devil makes a point with a loud snarl.

to share information. Communication helps animals find mates, locate family members, challenge rivals, defend territory, find food, and warn of danger.

WHAT IS SOUND?

Sound is a form of energy. It is created from vibrations moving through a medium, or substance. The medium can be a solid, a liquid, or a gas. Vibrations cause particles in the medium to bump into one another. This creates movement called a sound wave. Sound waves travel until they run out of energy.

Sound waves travel differently in different mediums. For example, sound travels four times faster in water than it does in air. That is because water is denser than air. Its particles are more closely packed.

Frequency is the number of times a particle moves back and forth when a sound wave passes through it. The sensation of frequency is

Geese make high-pitched sounds that travel well over water and open land.

commonly referred to as **pitch**. Low-pitched sounds are made by low-frequency sound waves. Low-pitched sounds can travel farther than high-pitched sounds, because the sound waves are longer. They can go around obstacles without scattering, because they lose less energy as they travel.

Animals that live in forests tend to produce lower-pitched sounds. Their sounds can be heard through the trees and brush. Animals that live in open areas such as grasslands create higher-pitched sounds because there are few obstacles in the way.

Wind can alter sound waves. It can keep sound from traveling as far as it would in still air. It can also make sound travel farther, depend-

Howler monkeys make an even bigger noise if they join a friend.

ing on the direction in which it is blowing. That is why many animals are most vocal between dusk and dawn, when the air tends to be more still.

The howler monkey is one of the loudest mammals in the world, thanks to a specialized bone in its throat. Every morning, a howler monkey calls out as it moves through the rain forest. This lets other monkeys know where it is so they can avoid an unplanned confrontation. A howler monkey's roaring call carries several miles through the forest.

A DOG WITH ANTLERS?

The muntjac of southern China and Taiwan is known as the "barking deer" because it barks like a dog when it senses danger. The male has tusklike upper teeth that grow to be about 1 inch (2.5 centimeters long. That's much longer than the teeth of other kinds of deer. *Woof!*

WORKING TOGETHER

The meerkat is a kind of mongoose that lives in the desert. Many meerkat families live together in a huge community of twenty to fifty or more individuals. The group posts lookout sentries throughout the colony of burrows. These guards keep an eye open for predators, such as hawks, owls, jackals, and snakes. The sentries stand erect, balancing on their long tails. They keep watch so the other meerkats can forage for food, groom, and play. If danger is spotted, one shrill bark sends all the meerkats scrambling for their burrows.

COOPERATION

Sometimes animals benefit from the alarm calls made by animals of different species. The Diana monkey shares its forested domain with a bird called the African hornbill. The Diana monkey sounds different alarms, depending on the specific danger. If the call warns of a leopard in the area, most hornbills don't react, since they can easily avoid a leopard attack. However, if the call warns of an eagle—an enemy of both the monkey and the bird—flying overhead, the hornbills will rush for cover.

Diana monkeys let everyone know if danger is lurking.

CHAPTER TWO

LOVE SONGS

On the island of Borneo in Southeast Asia, a male tree frog searches the forest for just the right place to sing his song. He finds a water-filled hole in a tree and climbs inside. Then he begins to peep. He raises and lowers the pitch of his peeps until the water-filled hole **resonates** with his mating song. This animal display of "singing in the shower" will cause female Borneo tree frogs to come looking to mate.

The Borneo tree frog sings from inside a hole in a tree branch.

Animals that live in communities usually have little trouble finding mates. Animals that live more solitary lives have to go to more trouble to team up with partners. Vocalizing is one way to attract attention. It is usually the male that makes all the racket.

Looking for love can be dangerous. Many hopeful males are tracked by their songs and gobbled up by predators. A male cicada has one of the loudest songs in the world. This insect has a pair of organs on its belly called **tymbals**. The tymbals can be clicked in and out, like the metal lids on glass food jars. Air sacs under the tymbals make the sound louder. The male cicada does his singing while hidden in bushes, trees, or grasses. The female cicada carefully tracks down a potential mate by following his tune.

TYMBALS

Some cicadas can be heard from 1 mile (1.5 kilometers) away.

SPRING SINGERS

Hearing a chorus of songbirds in the morning is one of the first signs that spring has arrived.

Many of these musical masters are not born with songs in their heads. They learn from their fathers and neighbors. In the spring the male songbird bursts into song, competing with other males in the area. The female bird carefully picks out her favorite crooner to start a family with. Then dad teaches the little chicks all of his favorite songs.

A male warbler sings for a mate.

SONG AND DANCE

Male capercaillies of the forests of Asia and northern Europe also gather in one area to attract mates. The males start off by fanning their tails and calling from high in the trees. After a while, and especially when females show up, the males jump to the forest floor. Then each one claims a small piece of land as a display stage. The

A male capercaillie sings from a stage.

females choose the birds with the best displays. Sometimes fights break out as the males carry out their courtship ritual.

BUBBLE LOVE

What isn't to love about a scaly, toothy needle-nosed crocodilian? The gharial is a critically endangered crocodilian from India and Nepal. The male has a bulb at the end of his long, skinny snout. He uses the bulb

Singing Fish

A funny-looking fish called the plainfin midshipman of the Pacific Ocean has its own special love song. The male can hum, whistle, growl, and grunt. The hum sounds like a foghorn that can sometimes be heard above water. A bunch of humming males can sound like a swarm of bees or a motorboat race.

Male gharial reptiles sing through their noses.

to make a loud, buzzing noise to attract female gharials. He can also blow bubbles with the bulb, which females seem to find very alluring.

Another critter uses bubbles to impress the females. The male ruddy duck has an air sac hidden in his chest feathers. Dense feathers trap the air until the duck beats on his chest with his beautiful blue beak. The loud slapping drumroll, the burst of bubbles his drumming produces, and the croaking sound of the air sac as it deflates all make an impressive love song.

A male humpback whale that has attracted a female partner might release a long stream of bubbles through his blowhole. He is trying to prevent other males from spotting his new friend and stealing her away.

Owls are crooners of the night.

SING-ALONG

It's not always males that make all the noise. Sometimes female animals join in the singing. The male tawny owl will *hooo huhuhuhuhooo* as a way to attract a female in the woodlands of Eurasia. Sometimes a female will answer with *ke-wick!* When the male hears her response, he usually brings her a bite to eat. Smart move!

The siamang is a gibbon from Indonesia that is very vocal, like most forest-dwelling primates. Its calls are louder than most because of a throat sac that can inflate like a balloon. The sac helps to boost the sound and make it last longer when the ape sings. The songs are often duets sung by a male and female that have joined together. Sometimes they each get a solo, and sometimes other members of the family will join in the singing. Scientists believe that the communal singing helps to strengthen the family bond.

Siamong gibbons have inflatable throats much like frogs.

MASTER CROONERS

Deep in the ocean, another creature moans a melody. A humpback whale's song can last twenty minutes and travel more than 20 miles (32 km). Nobody is quite sure how the humpback makes the sounds, because whales do not have vocal cords, no air escapes as they sing, and their mouths do not move. The other mystery is the reason for the music. Some scientists think the humpbacks are singing love songs. Others think the tunes are territorial.

The master of love crooners might be the lyrebirds of Australia. They get their name from the shape of the male's tail when he displays it. His outer feathers are white and brown, like the frame of a musical harplike instrument called a lyre. The fine, wispy, inner tail features look like the strings of the lyre.

Fast Fact

Early recordings of the humpback whale were made by a marine scientist named Roger Payne. *Songs of the Humpback Whale* was released as a record album in 1970, helping to change the way people looked at the animal kingdom.

A male lyrebird displays as he sings.

The male lyrebird builds a stage from dirt and then stands on it, spreading his beautiful, long tail feathers over his head. Then he sings songs he has developed from a collection of songs and sounds he has heard around him, even sounds such as car horns and chain saws. As if his musical arrangement isn't impressive enough, the lyrebird also dances as he sings. Look out, girls!

CHAPTER THREE

GET LOST!

Many animals have sounds they use to claim and defend their territory. The ear-splitting roar from a male lion that spreads across the Serengeti tells the world that this is his land and other male lions better keep away. Lions live in groups called prides and fiercely defend their

A male lion is on the alert even when it is resting.

family group and territory. The female lion is the one who is really in charge of the pride, even though it is the male lion who makes most of the racket.

Some animals also use sound to warn a possible attacker to back off. Members of the cat family will hiss, yeow, and even make a loud spitting sound to surprise an attacker and hopefully scare it away. This behavior is called antipredator signaling. Many times it is just a bluff, however, the message is clear: stay away, or I could hurt you!

NOISY CRAWLERS

Tarantulas and other big spiders can also hiss like cats. If one of these spiders feels threatened, it rears up and rubs the hairs on its front legs together. This act, called stridulating, creates a raspy noise. The spider will keep making the hissing sound until the danger has passed.

A hissing spider is one to avoid.

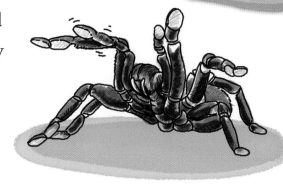

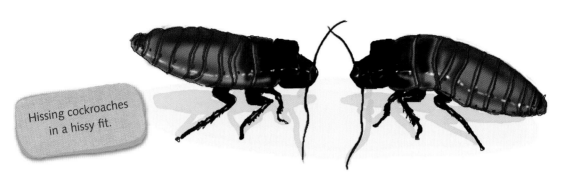

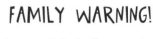
Hissing cockroaches in a hissy fit.

While spiders and some insects such as grasshoppers rub together body parts to make a hissing sound, the hissing cockroach from Madagascar actually expels air through the breathing holes in its body to make a loud hissing sound. The 2- to 3-inch (5- to 7.6-centimeter) giant insect usually hisses when fighting with another hissing cockroach. The best hisser wins.

FAMILY WARNING!

A large bird from Australia called the laughing kookaburra is also called "the bushman's clock." Almost every evening at dusk and every morning

A kookaburra chorus.

at dawn, kookaburra family members will join in to sing a chorus of crazy laughter that sounds like *kook-kook-kook-ka-ka-ka!* They are most likely making sure their territory is safe and secure. What predators could put up with all that racket?

Gorillas have a reputation for beating on their chests to look powerful. An adult male gorilla may try to ward off another gorilla by standing up and slapping his chest while he roars and screams. He presents himself as being very intimidating and hopes that it works. Normally, gorillas are quiet, peaceful animals.

The Tasmanian devil of Australia is not a quiet, peaceful animal much of the time. The Looney Tunes cartoon version of a very cranky creature roaring around like a snarling tornado is not far from the truth. A Tasmanian

Gorillas are peaceful unless they feel threatened.

GO AWAY!

There is a bird in South Africa that yells *kay-waaaay!* in a very loud voice when it sees danger from high in a tree. It is aptly called the go-away bird.

Tasmanian devils eat food they can find, such as the bones of a dead animal.

devil will launch into a screeching rage if it feels threatened in any way. It doesn't like anyone to mess with its food, especially another Tasmanian devil. The Tasmanian devil is a scavenger that sniffs out dead stuff. Loud shrieks and screams ring out in the night if a group of them argues over a carcass. Usually, nobody gets hurt in these noisy battles.

GUARD DUTY

Coyotes travel and live together in groups called packs, but they usually roam their territory alone as they search for food. They stay in touch with one another by barking and howling. Barks are used to locate one another. Long howls carry farther and are used for sending special messages. This regular communication lets any outsider know that this is their territory, so keep out!

Songbirds can also be very vocal when it comes to defending their territory, including their food supplies and nesting sites. Many of the beautiful, melodic songs we hear from male birds are actually threats of violence against potential invaders. A male songbird will even copy a neighboring male's song, as if he is mocking him. Usually, these guys are only warning off birds of the same species, since they would eat the same foods, choose the same kind of nesting site, and be interested in the same females.

Fast Fact

The North American brown thrasher is estimated to sing more than two thousand different songs.

CHAPTER FOUR

BABY TALK

Deep inside a cave, millions of baby bats cluster together to keep warm. Throughout the night, mother bats fly into the cave to feed their hungry babies. A mother locates her single baby among the millions by its own special squeak and smell.

Finding one baby in a huge crowd is not very easy for humans, but it is part of life for many other animals. Sea lion mothers and their pups live in a nursery colony called a **rookery**. When the mom comes back after going out for food, she trumpets loudly. Her pup will recognize her and bleat back to her. Sea lions also use smell and sight to find each other.

A mother penguin listens for the call of her pup.

King penguin babies huddle together in their rookeries in the cold temperatures of the Antarctic, waiting for their parents to return from feeding. Tens of thousands of babies might be squawking at the same time, but the parents can recognize their own chick's special call.

FAMILY COMMUNICATION

For many animals there are lots of ways parents communicate with their young. A mother duck has an assembly call for her ducklings that gets them to line up and follow her. A soft contentment call can be heard coming from the paddling chicks, and mom might even join in. Elephant babies are believed to make a purring noise when they feel safe and secure.

Bottlenose dolphins are very social animals with a huge variety of whistles

Baby ducks get in line when mom calls!

25

and squeaks that they use to talk to one another. Dolphin calves develop their own unique whistles very early in life. They learn by listening to their parents and other members of the pod. Some scientists believe these whistles are like the names we call one another, except no two seem to be the same. The whistles can be outside the range of human hearing. Dolphins also make sounds that humans can hear, such as barking, bleating, squealing, snapping, moaning, and groaning.

MOMMA TALK

A crocodile mom is gentle with her babies.

Baby Nile crocodiles from Africa start talking before they even hatch from their eggs. *Umph! umph! umph!* can be heard from the eggs a mother crocodile has buried in the sandy riverbank. Researchers believe the calls babies make are messages to one another and to their mother that they are about to hatch. The mother crocodile hears the calls and digs up the eggs to help her babies get free. She will also gently bite open unhatched eggs and then carry the tiny babies in her jaws to the safety of the water.

Most animal babies learn to be quiet once they are out in the wild, including baby black bears. However, a baby black bear is very chatty when it is safe in the den with its siblings and mom. It will cry to let Mom know when it tumbles away from her. She will find the cub and push it back to her warm belly. A different crying sound lets Mom know that it can't find her milk. Sometimes it will make a special cry when it is frustrated by being so small and helpless. People who study bear nurseries have also recorded a unique sound bear cubs make when they are nursing. They hum! If there are two or three cubs humming at once, it can be very noisy in that bear cave.

Fast Fact

People use special calls that sound like young animals in distress in order to attract animals. Some of them are hunters, but others are people who study animal behavior.

A bear den filled with cubs can be a noisy place.

CHAPTER FIVE

SHAKE, RATTLE, AND DRUMROLL

illions of animals have unique ways to communicate. Animals can use their bodies and special abilities to create a multitude of sounds in a variety of amazing ways.

A rattlesnake does not need a voice to warn off an attacker that confronts it. This North American snake has a bunch of hollow rings at the end of its tail. It can shake its tail to produce a rattling sound. If the attacker doesn't heed this warning, the rattler can strike with poisonous fangs.

The rattle of a rattlesnake is a fair warning to get away!

The Cape porcupine of South Africa doesn't have a poisonous bite, but it will shake its tail if it feels threatened. Its tail has hollow spines that make a rattling noise if shaken. The noise warns any potential attacker, "Hey, these pointy things can hurt you!"

WILD DRUMMERS

Drumming is a very popular way for some animals to let other animals know what's happening. Chimpanzees will drum on trees with their hands and feet as they travel through the forest. Scientists think they are letting their friends know where they are and which way they are going. The sounds can be heard by humans from about a half mile (0.8 km) away.

Chimpanzes use drumming to communicate.

A male ruffed grouse drums its wings on a hollow log.

A woodpecker can use its beak as a drumstick. It will tap on trees to claim its territory. Woodpeckers sometimes try to choose an instrument that broadcasts the biggest sound—such as a hard metal flagpole. Ouch!

Bird wings can also drum out a rhythm. The ruffed grouse is a large bird that spends most of its time on forest floors. The male grouse can make a drumming sound by compressing air under its wings and flapping. It sometimes drums while perching on a hollow log. The air in the log helps boost the sound, making it travel farther and last longer.

Fish know how to drum, too. Scientists are discovering many unique ways that fish create noise to attract mates and scare away predators. Many of them twitch their swim bladders back and forth to make noise. The butter-

Feathery Instruments

Researchers found that the chirps and beeps made by the male Anna's hummingbird while diving don't come from its mouth or wings but from its tail feathers. The sound is part of a display to attract a female and to warn other male hummers or predators to stay away.

fly fish uses its swim bladder to make a whispering sound. Maybe butterfly fish swim very close together so they can hear one another talking!

UNDERWATER NOISE

A noisy, small sea creature called the snapping shrimp has one oversized claw that looks sort of like a boxing glove. The shrimp makes a *pop-crack*ing sound by opening the claw and snapping it shut. The sound waves the shrimp produces are powerful enough to stun or kill its prey. Researchers discovered that when the claw shuts, a water jet shoots out at speeds up to 62 miles (100 km) an hour. The wake of the jet stream leaves behind a bubble that pops with a loud bang. They also discovered that a flash of light also occurs when the bubble bursts. When a colony of snapping shrimp start clacking their claws, submarines in the area can avoid being detected by sonar.

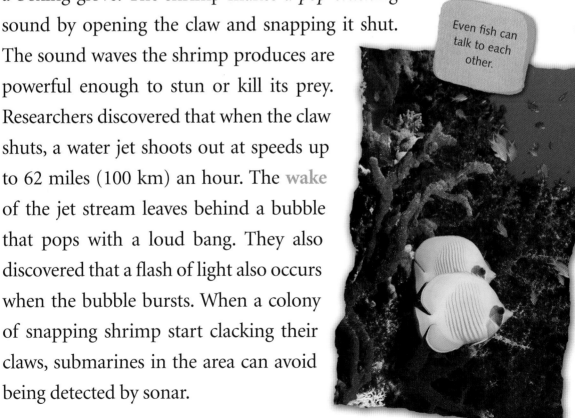

Even fish can talk to each other.

CHAPTER SIX
SOUNDS OF SILENCE

T here are lots of quiet ways animals can communicate, for the same reasons other animals scream, sing, and create other kinds of racket.

A wolf has an effective way to communicate without making noise, even though it can bark, whine, and howl. A wolf gestures with its tail. A tail raised high signals that the wolf is in charge. A wolf with a lowered tail is saying that it is submissive. Other animals in the dog family also use their tails

Wolves know their place in the pack. The wolf in the illustration on the left is not in charge, so its tail is lowered. The wolf in the illustration on the right is in charge. It carries its tail high.

to talk. Some tails, such as those of the fox, dingo, and jackal, have a black or white tip on the end. The tip color may help make it easier to see if the tail is up or down. Good information to know!

Other animals also use tail talk. When a white-tailed deer spots danger, it raises its fluffy white tail. The white flash can be seen across a field or forest and warns the others in the herd to watch out. The white tail also lets the predator know it has been spotted.

The sun-tailed monkey is from Gabon, a country in west-central Africa. It gets its name from its long, white tail with a yellow-orange tip. The male in charge keeps his tail raised high as the monkeys in his troop travel through the dense rain forest. That way the other monkeys can see where he goes and follow along.

A sun-tailed monkey's tail is easily spotted in the grass.

BODY TALK

The way an animal uses its body also sends signals to others. Animals use complicated body language to express themselves. An elephant that flares its ears and shakes its trunk is angry and might be about to charge. A cat that arches its back with the hair standing up feels threatened. When a hippo tosses back its head and yawns, watch out! Yawning is not necessarily a sign that an animal is sleepy. The baboon and other primates appear to yawn as a way to threaten a potential enemy or to show anxiety. The guinea pig yawns as a way to show off its powerful teeth. Many lizards and snakes open their mouths wide as a warning. Other animals, such as male Adélie penguins of Antarctica, yawn as part of a courtship ritual.

A hippo will yawn if it is angry.

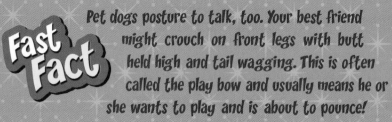
Fast Fact Pet dogs posture to talk, too. Your best friend might crouch on front legs with butt held high and tail wagging. This is often called the play bow and usually means he or she wants to play and is about to pounce!

The honeybee uses an amazing form of body language to pass messages to the members of its hive. She uses a "waggle dance" to tell other bees how to locate a rich source of flowers where they can gather pollen and nectar. When a worker bee returns to the hive with pollen and nectar, she starts dancing on the vertical surface of the comb. The dance is usually in a figure-eight pattern. She waggles her body from side to side as she dances in a straight line. The dance tells the others which way to go and how far to fly.

The chimpanzee has a variety of facial expressions it uses to communicate. Its flexible lips let it make a variety of faces that tell if it is scared, upset, or feeling playful. An adult male gorilla will bulge out his lower lip, stand stiff-legged, and stare hard at an intruder if he feels that his harem is being threatened. Good time to back off!

TOUCH TALK

Animals that hang out in close-knit communities, such as gorillas and chimpanzees, also use touch to communicate. They hug, scratch, lick, groom, and even lean on each other. This direct way of communicating is a form of bonding with one another. Animals such as lions and zebras nuzzle and groom each other as a show of affection, as well as a way to scratch those hard-to-reach spots. Chimpanzees that are close buddies will often kiss each other when they meet.

Elephants use their trunks to touch and embrace their family members. Old relations who meet up after a while apart will use their trunks to "shake hands." Adult elephants touch each other with their trunks and even entwine their trunks as a sign of affection. Babies receive trunk caresses from all the adult females or a rub from a foot

Fast Fact

Almost all animals on the planet can pass along messages to others of their kind using chemical communication.

as a sign of affection and reassurance. The baby can also be slapped by an adult's trunk as a way to say, "Stop that!"

Insects that live in large colonies, such as termites, have a silent chemical vocabulary. Each termite colony has its own identifying chemical passed to its members by the queen mother. No termites without that smell are allowed in the nest. The nest can have millions of brothers and sisters living in it.

Pheromones are chemicals that animals release to transmit messages. The pheromones released by the queen assign duties to the termites, such as cleaning and repairing the nest, caring for the young, finding food and water, fighting attackers, and constructing new tunnels and rooms for the growing termite family.

Elephants use their trunks to "talk."

The inside of a termite mound is bustling with activity.

CHAPTER SEVEN

YOU LIGHT UP MY LIFE

Many animals have special features in or on their bodies that help them to communicate in some amazing ways. Scientists have discovered that many animals can see colors. Some animals, especially birds such as peacocks, use color as a way to communicate. The peacock has a beautiful tail that it uses to "talk." When he spreads his huge tail train, the colorful feathers arch into a wide fan that can touch the ground on either side. No words are necessary.

The frilled lizard, from the dry forests of Australia and New Guinea, gets its name from the

A male peacock shows off its beautiful tail.

big flap of skin attached to its neck. During breeding season, a male frilled lizard will fan out his frill, like a peacock fans out his tail, and show off the bright yellow and orange colors. If another male offers

to battle, both will show off their frills and open their big yellow or pink mouths.

Male frilled lizards will try and out frill each other as a type of battle.

The hooded seal, from the far northern Atlantic Ocean, looks like a plain gray-and-black-spotted seal. When a male hooded seal wants to show off his power, he uses a special body part to communicate his aggressive intentions. The nasal cavity in the adult male becomes enlarged, forming a flap of skin. Usually the flap just hangs in front of the seal's upper lip. But when he needs to send the message that he is one tough guy, he can force air into the flap until it blows up into a big, reddish pink balloon. Then he shakes it around to create a pinging sound. This display is

Hooded seals have built-in balloons.

used as a sign of aggression toward other males. It's also a warning to other males to stay away during breeding season.

The firefly, or lightning bug, is a beetle that can glow. It uses its blinking light to attract a mate. Some female fireflies have no wings. They will climb on a leaf or twig and check out the blinking male fireflies that are flying around. The language of fireflies is based on different patterns of flashes. When a female firefly sees a flash signal she likes, she gives that male a special female flash signal and waits for him to come and find her.

RAINBOW IN THE SEA

Sea creatures come in a rainbow of colors and patterns. However, some of them can change their looks. Octopuses, squid, and cuttlefish belong to a group of animals called cephalopods. Many cephalopods have the amazing ability to alter their skin color and patterning. They use this skill to signal warnings, blend in with their surroundings to hide from predators and prey, and show off for potential mates.

The squid is a quick-change artist that changes its color as a way to communicate. It has special cells in its skin called **chromatophores**. The squid controls its skin color by squeezing the muscles around the chromatophores so only certain ones show at a given time. It can use color to greet a potential mate, and it can tell a potential

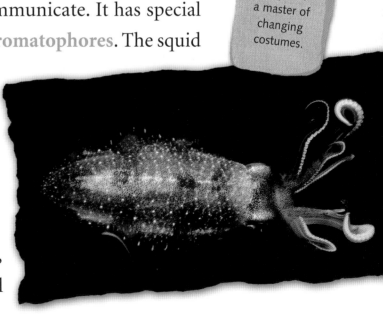

A squid is a master of changing costumes.

Jelly fish show off their colors.

attacker that it is ready to defend itself.

The squid also has the ability to emit light, as do many creatures in the sea. Almost all marine animals emit light as a way to find one another, scare off predators, and lure food in the darkness of the ocean. The light is made from energy released during a chemical reaction in different parts of the animals' bodies. The millions of blinking, sparking, dancing, twirling lights are like an underwater light show!

ZAPPY TALK

Other sea creatures communicate by using electricity. All sea animals have a faint electrical field around them. Since water is a good conductor of electricity, fish can communicate by sensing the electric currents of everything around them. Some send electrical signals to communicate with their friends and family. The bad news is, sharks can detect these signals. Sharks have an amazing ability to locate a tasty snack simply by homing in on the electrical signals the animal emits. Sharks' snouts are covered with receptors that can detect the tiniest amount of electricity.

All animals have some way to communicate. It can be a buzz, a look, a chemical, a flash of light, a color, or a blood-curdling scream. Communicating is probably the most important skill an animal possesses. Without a way to communicate, it would be very tough for animals, including humans, to survive.

GLOSSARY

bioluminescence the production and giving off of light by a living thing

chromatophore a cell that has color and light-reflecting properties

communal of or relating to a community

conductor a material that allows electricity to flow freely

domain land that is controlled by an individual

frequency the rate of a wave's vibration

harem a group of females associated with one male

medium a substance through which signals can travel

pheromone a chemical substance released by an animal that effects the behavior of others

pitch the property of sound that varies with frequency

resonate to increase vocal sound by using the vibration of air in certain cavities and bony structures

rhythm a regular, repeated pattern of movement or sound

rookery a breeding place or colony

sentries soldiers that stand guard

stridulating producing a sound by rubbing together certain body parts

submissive humbly obedient

swim bladders air-filled sacs in fish that help them maintain their position in the water

tymbals the part of a cicada that vibrates and makes noise

wake the wave that spreads about behind something that moves in water

FIND OUT MORE

Books

Animals: A Visual Encyclopedia. New York: DK
    Publishing, 2008.

McGhee, Karen, and George McKay. *National
    Geographic Encyclopedia of Animals.* Washington,
    D.C.: National Geographic Children's Books, 2006.

Uhlenbroek, Charlotte. *Animal Life.* New York: DK
    Publishing, 2008.

Websites

Animal Diversity Web
http://animaldiversity.ummz.umich.edu/site/index.html

Animal Planet
http://animal.discovery.com

eNature: America's Wildlife Resource
http://enature.com/home

National Geographic Kids
http://kids.nationalgeographic.com/kids

INDEX

Pages in boldface are illustrations.

ABOUT THE AUTHOR

ROBIN KOONTZ grew up in a wild suburb of Maryland and later lived in West Virginia. She learned from some great people how to respect every living creature. Robin now lives with her husband and various critters in the Coast Range mountains of western Oregon. She shares her office space with spiders and whatever they happen to catch.